TASTY LEMON CURD

Zoey Laurent

PREFACE OF THE PUBLISHER

We are pleased that you have chosen this book.
If you are in possession of a paperback book, we will
gladly send you the same as an e-book, then you can
easily turn the pages digitally as well as normally.

We attach great importance to the fact that all of
our authors, when creating their own cookbooks,
have recooked all of their recipes several times.
Therefore, the quality of the design of the
recipes and the instructions for recooking
are detailed and will certainly succeed.

Our authors strive to optimize your recipes,
but tastes are and will always be different!

We at Mindful Publishing support the creation
of the books, so that the creative authors of the
recipes can take their time and enjoy cooking.

We appreciate your opinion about our recipes,
so we would appreciate your review of the book
and your experience with these great recipes!

In order to reduce the printing costs of our books and to offer the possibility to offer recipes in books at all, we have to do without pictures in the cookbooks. The digital version has the same content as the paperback.

Our recipes will convince you and reveal to you a culinary style you can't get enough of!

Enough of the foreword, let the recipes begin!

MERINGUE CUPCAKES WITH LEMON CURD FILLING

difficult

Ingredients

100g of soft butter
100g powdered sugar
100g of flour
1 teaspoon of yeast
2 eggs
1 zest of treated lemongrass

Preparation

Cupcake preparation:
Preheat the oven to 180°C (thermostat 6).
In a bowl, mix the softened butter (especially
not melted!) with the sugar, then add the
eggs, flour and baking powder.

Then add the zest and juice of the
lemons to the dough.
Divide into 12 small moulds 7 cm in
diameter and 3 or 4 cm high, then bake for
20 minutes at 180°C (thermostat 6).
Preparation of the Lemon Curd :
Put all the ingredients in a glass bowl and mix.
Place the bowl on a pan of simmering water
without the bottom of the bowl touching
the water, and stir until the sugar melts.
Continue cooking over low heat, stirring
constantly: it may take 20 minutes
(but the result is delicious)!
The cream is ready when it coats the back of
the spoon (it should be relatively thick).
Caution: the cream must not boil or the
eggs will turn into scrambled eggs.
Let cool then fill the cupcakes from which
you will have removed the cap and dug
the equivalent of a small spoon.
Preparation of the Meringue :
Mix the egg white and sugar in a bowl
and put in a bain marie.
Whisk by hand for a few minutes until the sugar is
dissolved and then remove from the water bath.
Beat with an electric whisk at medium
speed for 10 minutes.
Add the lemon juice and beat at high
speed until the mixture forms peaks that
hold when you remove the whisk.

Spread over the cupcakes and brown with a torch. Decorate as you wish!

LEMON CURD FINANCIER

easy

Ingredients

100g of sugar
125g of hazelnut powder
2 eggs
80g of butter
2 tablespoons of flour
1 pot of lemon curd (bought or homemade)

Preparation

Preheat the oven to 180°C (thermostat 6).
Mix the sugar and the hazelnut powder
then add the eggs.
Add 60 g of butter beforehand melted,
mix and add the flour, stir well in order
to obtain a homogeneous paste.
Butter the moulds with the remaining butter. Pour
the paste in small moulds until half height then
put a small teaspoon of lemon curd in the center.

Bake for 12 minutes

LEMON CURD IN THE MICROWAVE

very easy

Ingredients

10cl of lemon juice (about 3 lemons)
lemon peel
160g of sugar
3 eggs
1 tablespoon of cornstarch
40g of butter

Preparation

Mix all the ingredients homogeneously.
Place in a microwave-safe dish 3 x 1 minute on
high (750W), stirring after each minute.
Now it's ready, a real delight.
Use it to garnish tarts, to fill a cake or simply
on its own...

LEMON CURD FONDANT RAMEKIN

easy

Ingredients

120g lemon curd + 4 teaspoons of lemon
3 eggs
80g of sugar
35g of butter
1 tablespoon of flour

Preparation

Preheat the oven to 210°C (gas mark 7), melt
the butter and add it to the 120 g of lemon
curd to make a homogeneous paste.
In a bowl, mix the eggs, sugar and flour.
Then add the lemon curd preparation and mix.
Pour 1/3 of the preparation in individual ramekins.
Add in each one 1 teaspoon of lemon
curd. then cover with the preparation.

Place the ramekins in the oven for about 12 minutes.

LEMON YOGHURT ON A BED OF LEMON CURD

easy

Ingredients

1l whole milk
1 natural yogurt
200g of sugar
2 sachets of vanilla sugar
Lemon aroma

Preparation

Prepare the yoghurt by mixing the milk,
powdered sugar and vanilla sugar. Add a few
drops of lemon flavouring. Set aside.
Prepare the lemon curd by taking the zest of 2
lemons. Recover the juice of the 4 lemons.
Put in a saucepan the zests and juice of the
lemons, the sugar and finally the cornflour.
Heat on low heat and add the eggs.

Stir continuously until the mixture thickens.
Leave to cool and put a layer of lemon curd
at the bottom of each yoghurt pot and fill
the pot with the yoghurt preparation.
Turn on the yoghurt maker and leave it on
overnight (between 10 and 12 hours).
Then put your jars in the fridge for at
least 4 hours before tasting.

LEMON CURD PIE

easy

Ingredients

1 puff pastry
1 pot of lemon curd
2 lemons
150g powdered sugar
1 tablespoon of liquid vanilla
1/2l of water

Preparation

Bake the puff pastry in a pie tin (in the oven at
180°C, thermostat 6, for 10 to 15 min).
Melt the sugar in water in a saucepan.
Add the vanilla.
Bring this syrup to the boil for about 15 min.
Cut the lemons into thin slices.
Add them to the syrup.
Let poach gently for 20 min.
Once the lemons are candied, drain them.
Reserve the syrup.
Garnish the tart with the lemon curd.
Arrange the slices of lemons on the tart.

Coat the tart with the syrup (if necessary, put it back on the heat for a few minutes to thicken it).

APPLE PIE WITH LEMON CURD

easy

Ingredients

1 pie dough (broken, shortbread or puff pastry)
4 apples
50g of raisins (optional)
3 egg whites
1 honey
1 cinnamon
2 lemon curd (recipe for cooking pot)
1 brown sugar if not available)
10cl of cream at 15% fat
Lemon

Preparation

Peel the apples and cut them in half, lemon them.
Mix the honey with half of the cinnamon and the cut
apples in a salad bowl, and microwave for 5 minutes.
Spread the dough in a mould and bake for
10 minutes at 180°C (gas mark 6).

During this time, whip the 3 egg whites
with the spoonful of vergoise, the rest of
cinnamon, the liquid cream, the lemon
curd and the grapes if you put some.
Once this is done, spread the soft apples in the pie
crust and pour the egg white mixture over it.
Cook the tart in the oven at 180°C
(thermostat 6), 20 to 25 min.

LEMON CURD CAKE

easy

Ingredients

200g of flour
150g of sugar
75g of butter
4 eggs
Salt
1/2 packet of yeast

Preparation

Cookie :
Preheat the oven to 210°C (thermostat 7).
Whip the eggs with the sugar and salt on the fire.
When it is hot enough (too hot to put your
finger on), remove the mixture from the heat
then whisk to increase the volume.
Add the flour, yeast and melted butter.
Butter 2 flat moulds then fill them by dividing
the dough in 2 and making sure that

the dough is spread evenly.
Put in the oven for about 15 minutes.
Lemon Curd :
Grate the zest of the lemons in a container
and squeeze out the juice.
Melt the butter in a pan over very low heat.
Add the sugar and then the lemon zest and juice.
Beat the eggs in a bowl and pour them into the pan.
Stir continuously with a wooden spoon for
15 to 20 minutes until the dough thickens
(the eggs must not be cooked).
Finally, spread the lemon curd on the first
cake placed on a large dish (without letting
it drip next to it), cover with the second,
and pour the remaining over it.

LEMON CURD CHEESECAKE

easy

Ingredients

250g of shortbread cookie
125g of butter
750g of RAMOLLI cream cheese (type St Moret)
110g powdered sugar
half a lemon
3 eggs
1 pot of lemon curd

Some stores offer them in the English products section (a delicious recipe is available on this site).

Preparation

Crush the shortbread into fine crumbs.
I advise you to use your robot. Add the
butter without ceasing to stir.
Line the bottom and sides of a springform pan.
Cover and refrigerate 30 min at the coldest.
Preheat the oven to 170°, thermostat

6-7. Beat the cheese, sugar and zest with a
mixer. Beat in the eggs one by one.
Pour the mixture into the mould and cook
for 1 hour. When the cheesecake is firm,
let it cool to room temperature.
Spread the lemon curd on the cake. Refrigerate
at least 3 hours, even overnight. Unmould
just before serving.
Enjoy!

MASCARPONE AND LEMON CURD CHEESECAKE

Average level

Ingredients

250g of mascarpone
2 eggs
1 sachet of vanilla sugar
140g of sugar
1 tablespoon of cornstarch
4 lemons not treated
1 sheets of gelatin
200g of English cookie digestive type
100g of melted butter

Preparation

Prepare the lemon curd :
Put in a saucepan 2 lemon zests, the
juice of 3 lemons and 100 g of sugar.
Heat and add the cornflour.

In a bowl, beat 2 egg yolks, lower the heat of the saucepan and add them to the syrup. Whip the mixture until it thickens. Keep in a cool place.

For the dough:

Melt the butter. Crush the cookies (I put them in a freezer bag and crush them with a rolling pin) and add the butter. Line the bottom of a springform pan with the dough and let cool.

For the cream:

Whip the mascarpone with the vanilla sugar and 40 g of sugar. Beat the 2 remaining whites until stiff and add them to the mascarpone. For the holding, dissolve a sheet of gelatine in the juice of a lemon previously heated and incorporated into this cream.

Assembly:

Spread the lemon curd on the cookie and cover with the mascarpone cream. Ideally keep in a cool place overnight.

LEMON CURD WITH ENGLISH LEMON CURD

easy

Ingredients

2 lemons
50g of butter
150g of sugar
2 eggs + 1 yolk

Preparation

Cut the butter into cubes and set aside.
Whisk the eggs, sugar and lemon juice together
with a whisk so that it aerates the cream
without weighing it down.
Cook in a bain-marie, stirring continuously
for 20 minutes.
Remove from the bain-marie and leave to cool for
a few moments, the top should still be warm.
Incorporate the butter and stir with a spatula.

Fill a jar with jam and place a plastic film directly on the cream to avoid the formation of a skin on the surface. Keep in a cool place.

LEMON CURD WITH GRAPEFRUIT AND CLEMENTINE

easy

Ingredients

3 organic yellow lemons
2 clementines
1 grapefruit blight
2 tablespoons of flour
4 eggs
150g of sugar

Preparation

Zest 1 lemon and cut the zest into small
pieces of about 1 cm wide.
Squeeze all the fruit.
Put the pieces of zest, fruit juice, sugar and flour
in a saucepan, put on low heat and stir regularly.
In the meantime, beat the eggs and
add them to the mixture.

Increase the heat regularly while stirring the mixture vigorously without stopping until it thickens. The goal is to avoid at most the solidification of eggs (small white pieces). If there are white pieces, pass the mixture through a sieve.

To put in pots.

To taste!

TIRAMISU WITH LEMON CURD

very easy

Ingredients

3 eggs
100g brown sugar
250g of mascarpone
24 cookies with a spoon
4 lemons
30g powdered sugar
10cl of limoncello
200g of homemade lemon curdmaison
made according to this recipe.

Preparation

Separate the whites from the yolks.
Mix the yolks with the brown sugar.
Add the mascarpone with a whisk.
Press two of the lemons. Add their juice to the
egg/sugar/mascarpone mixture. Whisk for a long
time to make the preparation homogeneous.

Whisk the egg whites until stiff and gently fold
them with a spatula into the previous mixture.
Squeeze two lemons. Add the 30 g of sugar
in the lemon juice. Add the limoncello.
Moisten the cookies in the sweetened
and flavoured lemon juice.
Line the bottom of the mould with the moistened
cookies. Cover them with half of the lemon curd.
Cover with a layer of cream, egg, sugar, mascarpone.
Make a new layer of moistened cookies,
then a layer of lemon curd. Finish with
a layer of mascarpone cream.
Put in the refrigerator for at least 12 hours.

LEMON CURD MUFFINS

very easy

Ingredients

3 eggs
150g of sugar
150g of soft butter
300g of flour
1 sachet of yeast
15cl of milk
Lemon curd (Marmiton recipe)

Preparation

Mix flour, sugar, baking powder.
Add the melted butter, eggs and milk.
Butter muffin tins and place a large tablespoon
of dough. Add a teaspoon of lemon curd and
cover with a tablespoon of dough.
Bake for 20 minutes in the oven at 180°C
(gas mark 6) and unmould.

ICED LEMON CURD

very easy

Ingredients

400g of lemon curd (recipe on site or in jar)
2 meringues (pastry or homemade)
600g curd cheese 20 % mg
150g of fresh raspberries (or coulis
according to season)

Preparation

Mix the lemon curd and fromage frais.
Crumble the meringues and incorporate
them into the preparation.
Fill the ramekins and place in the
freezer for 1 hour (minimum).
Take out 5 minutes before unmolding.
Place on small plates and decorate
with raspberries (or coulis).

MILLE FEUILLES MERINGUE LEMON CURD RASPBERRY

Average level

Ingredients

4 egg whites
250g of sugar

Preparation

Prepare the meringues the day before.
Preheat your oven to 110°C (thermostat 3-4).
Beat the egg whites until stiff and add the caster
sugar three times once the whites are well beaten.
Put the meringue in a piping bag with a fluted tip.
Make circles about 10cm in diameter on a
baking sheet covered with baking paper.
Put in the oven for 3 hours.
The next day:

The raspberry mousse :
Soak the gelatine leaves in cold
water (approx. 10 min).
Heat the raspberries in a saucepan.
Add the caster sugar.
Pass the preparation through a sieve to remove
the seeds and obtain a coulis, then heat it up
again for a few moments and melt the gelatine
that has been wrung out. Set aside.
Put your very cold liquid cream in a cul
de poule and whisk the cream.
Put part of the coulis in the whipped cream.
Mix well and repeat the operation
until the coulis is exhausted.
Put your mousse in the fridge so that it sets.
Once taken, put it in a piping bag with a
medium fluted tip and make small rosettes
around the meringue discs. Be careful to
keep 6 discs aside for the last floor.
The Lemon Curd:
Heat the pulco.
Mix the eggs with the sugar and the cornstarch.
Pour the hot pulco over the egg/sugar mixture.
Whisk and put back on low heat until thickened,
stirring with the whisk continuously so
that it doesn't stick to the bottom.
Once thickened, add the butter cut in small
pieces, mix well and reserve in the fridge.
Take the lemon curd out of the fridge.
Put it in a piping bag with a medium plain

tip and garnish the center of the meringues
up to the height of the raspberry rosettes
and assemble the mille-feuille.
Refrigerate until ready to serve.

LEMON CREAM (LEMON CURD)

Average level

Ingredients

4 medium sized lemons
150g of sugar
3 eggs
1 tablespoon of cornstarch

Preparation

Wash the lemons and in 'zester' 2, put
the very fine zests in a saucepan.
Squeeze the lemons and put the juice
with the zests in the pan.
Pour in the sugar and cornstarch.
Stir, and heat over low heat
Beat the eggs in a separate bowl.
Once the eggs are beaten, incorporate while stirring
the lemon juice, sugar, cornstarch and zest.
Put on strong fire and continue to stir with a whisk.
The mixture will start to thicken. Attention:

always stir when the eggs are added,
otherwise the lemon cream could burn!
Remove from the heat and put in jars (jam jars),
leave to cool and keep in the refrigerator.
Here are 3 minute recipe ideas for
using your lemon curd.
1- minute verrines: crumbled cookie,
lemon curd, crumbled meringue
2- minute tarts: Breton puck, lemon
curd, whipped cream
3- minute foam: emulsify the lemon
curd with whipped cream

LEMON CURD IN PRESSURE COOKER

very easy

Ingredients

4 egg trails
3 lemons + their zest
500g powdered sugar
125g of butter

Preparation

Use a pyrex-type bowl or bowl, which
can withstand high heat.
Remove the zest from the lemons. Extract
their juice and beat it with the whole eggs,
then add sugar, zests and soft butter.
Put water in the bottom of the pressure cooker,
then place the bowl with a plate upside down
on top to protect it from condensation.
Close the pressure cooker and when the

valve is released, turn down the heat
source and allow 10 minutes.
Take out the bowl and stir the preparation
to distribute the zests and put in the
previously scalded jars.
Can be kept for 6 weeks in the refrigerator.

SWEET SANDED LEMON CURD

very easy

Ingredients

4 Breton pallets
4 tablespoons lemon curd
4 meringues

Preparation

Arrange a Breton puck on a plate.
Put a tablespoon of Lemon curd on top.
Finish with a meringue.
Put in the fridge until serving time.

LEMON CURD

very easy

Ingredients

6 eggs
2 lemons or limes with zest
200g of sugar
100g of butter

Preparation

In a double boiler, beat the eggs and add the
lemon juice and zest, sugar and butter.
Cook, stirring constantly until it takes
the consistency of honey.
Put in a jar and keep in a cool place.

BIRTHDAY CAKE WITH LEMON CURD

easy

Ingredients

treated lemon peel
2 eggs
2 egg yolks
250g of sugar
100g of butter

Preparation

The day before prepare the lemon
curd and the cookie.
For the lemon curd: in a double boiler, mix the
sugar, the lemon juice and the eggs with a whisk.
Add the butter. To let thicken during
10 min while stirring.
To pass the lemon curd to the Chinese. Incorporate
the zests. To film and leave to the cool.

For the cookie, preheat the oven
to 180°, thermostat 6.
Mix butter and sugar. Add the flour and the
yeast. Then add the eggs, one by one.
Mix well the preparation, pour in a mould to
be missed and put in the oven for 45 min.
The same day, prepare the decoration.
Melt the marshmallow in 3 tablespoons
of water and a pinch of gel coloring.
Put in the bowl of a mixer. Gradually
add powdered sugar until you obtain a
consistency close to the dough.
Put powdered sugar on the work surface and
on the rolling pin and spread the dough.
Assembly of the birthday cake:
Cut the cookie in half.
Spread lemon curd on the first part of the cake.
Put the top of the cake back in place.
Spread the lemon curd all over the surface
of the cake and around the edges.
Place the marshmallow dough on
top of the cake and smooth.

IMPRINT

Mindful Publishing
We help you to publish your book!
By

TTENTION Inc.
Wilmington - DE19806
Trolley Square 20c

Instagram: mindful_publishing
Contact: mindful.publishing@web.de
Contact2: mindful.publishing@protonmail.com

Printed in Great Britain
by Amazon